T0003514

THE
Ultimate
DECEPTION

How God Created Man, and
How Man Invented God

BECHARA H. CHARBEL

Order this book online at www.trafford.com
or email orders@trafford.com

Most Trafford titles are also available at major online book retailers.

Printed in the United States of America.

ISBN: 978-1-4669-7061-8 (sc)
ISBN: 978-1-4669-7063-2 (hc)
ISBN: 978-1-4669-7062-5 (e)

Library of Congress Control Number: 2012922766

Trafford rev. 01/03/2013

 www.trafford.com

North America & international
toll-free: 1 888 232 4444 (USA & Canada)
phone: 250 383 6864 ♦ fax: 812 355 4082

CONTENTS

Preface and Dedication vii

1. Why are we here? 1

2. Some universal truths.. 6

3. The fallacies in religious teachings about God. 9

4. Why, then, did we all accept Religion? 13

5. What would you do if YOU were God? 16

6. The most difficult, yet the ONLY and logical decision:
   What would you have done if you were GOD? 25

7. How it all came into being.. 30

8. Would you have done it differently if YOU, were God?. . .32

9. This is why "WE" are here 36

PREFACE AND DEDICATION

God made me.

He gave me the power to think, question, believe, doubt, love, hate, invent, destroy, build, give life, even the power to kill, and every other imaginable power that he did not bestow on any other of his creations. Of all these powers God gave me, the ability to think and apply logic and deduction is the most precious gift God gave me. Even if my thinking was aimed at his nature and his intentions for the human race and all other creations.

I will not question to degrade, I will not doubt to debunk, and I will not waste this precious gift God gave me on simple speculation. I will use this gift to confirm and reaffirm that I am special, and if this was done for me, it was also done for each and every human being that ever lived, and that will ever live.

For those readers who do not believe that there is a God, the Creator of this universe and everything in it, perhaps reading this book will make them think about the logic that eventually will drive any rational creature to accept some form of God. Perhaps not necessarily in the practiced religious sense, but nevertheless a God who is all-encompassing, and who cares for all of us, believers as well as non-believers, in the same way parents care for their offspring, no matter what.

For those readers who have believed in the existence of God, whether by being taught religiously from their birth that God exists, or because they have adopted the belief in this certainty at a later stage in their life, I hope to confirm and reaffirm the soundness of their beliefs. Not in the same childish way we were all taught about God, but in a systematic observation that this universe is arranged and governed not only by immutable laws of physics, chemistry, dynamics, and biology. But more importantly that it is governed ultimately and forever by "Logic", pure an simple. But above all, this universe is governed, in a laissez-faire sort of way, by God.

If we make the assumption that God is the creator of all, we have to make the next deduction that God created all and everything in a "Logical" way, otherwise there will be no "Predictability" with any certainty to anything in this wonderful universe that God created. God will be forced to intervene constantly in the affairs of the universe, for ever, to keep bringing things into an order that can sustain all things and all creatures, with the most precious of these being Mankind. How much sense or logic does it make for an inventor to keep correcting or tweaking or guiding his invention, if this invention was created to "Excel", "Amaze", and otherwise provide the ultimate joy and satisfaction to its creator.

My objective in these writings is to reaffirm that God did indeed create this universe and the human race in such a wonderful way that he would not have or need to intervene, not even once, to perpetuate the wonderful "Experiment" we call "Mankind". And this by itself is the reason God created this universe and decided to disappear and not "Tinker" with it, ever.

Not only this, but I will go further to reaffirm that it would not make any sense for God to have created two of the same kind. Just as I believe and will prove that there is only one "Naturally" habitable planet, Earth.

Everything and anything that is in the universe has to make sense and has to follow the rule of logic. For people to explain unseen things or events or powers in any other way but the scientific and rational way, not only borders on heresy, but on lunacy. Or perhaps on a genius that figured things out but had no desire to share the "Truth" with the rest of us, as difficult as it may be to grasp by the average person.

In writing this book, I am not claiming to possess any special intellectual powers of thought or reasoning, beyond what each and every one of us has at birth. I have simply decided, after years of being raised as a Catholic Christian, and after observing and testing the multitude of hypotheses promulgated by the Christian Church (At least the one I was born and raised in) that, if any normal and rational person applied pure logical thinking to the eternal question as to why we exist on this earth, would have arrived at my same conclusions. Given my observation that, to my knowledge at the time of writing these words, no one has come out with a simplified way of explaining all this, and that most religions are still practiced and growing in numbers of their participants, I have come to conclude that someone has the duty to explain to the average human beings that they have been lied to, cheated, used, taken advantage of, misled, and otherwise had the proverbial wool pulled over their eyes for millennia.

In laying out my theories and conclusions, I am not by any means claiming that I have been spoken to by God, his messengers, angels, prophets, or any other unworldly being or thing. It is utterly inconceivable and absolutely illogical for God to choose only one of his creations to speak to and entrust with relaying his message to the rest of us. It just does not fit. Here, I am in no way accusing the prophets of making things up, or lying to us. I truly believe that they, too, have gone thru deep and uplifting inner thought and truly believed that their words and thoughts were from God (They could not accord themselves these powerful thoughts, being just human). Or perhaps they just fabricated the whole thing. Why not? As long as their intentions were good, and they only meant to persuade other people of lesser powers of thought and deduction to aspire to a higher power that is good and demands good behavior from its creations. There is no harm in what they have done. The true harm to humanity came later on, when charlatans and people with devious intentions took control, and never let go; More so, they passed on a twisted, erroneous and damaging set of rules and regulations that permeated most of society and resulted in wars, calamities, dissent and general divisiveness of all human beings, instead of uniting them for the most noble cause: Human well-being to accomplish God's mission for humanity.

Regardless of how and why there are so many people, prophets, and messiahs, past and yet-to-be, there can only be one truth about God. The explanations vary, the methods differ, and the practices surely are as divergent as can be, but the truth is ONE and only ONE.

It is with the spirit of oneness that I write these words to all of humanity, every single individual that was, is, and yet to be born, from every religion and belief and political affiliation, of all colors and ethnic origins. I hope everyone will be able to follow the simple rationale I am laying out in these pages and come to the conclusion that he or she is indeed a SPECIAL creation of God, endowed with all the special qualities a Creator gives to his Creations, and entrusted with demonstrating the beauty and special purpose for all human beings in the eyes and mind of their God.

I give special thanks to my lifetime friend Hamad for being so true to his faith, and for providing me with the initial spark to start me on this wonderful journey of self-examination and inward looking. And to finally put in words what has been roiling in my brain and heart for years, without me knowing what and why I had these feelings and thoughts.

I dedicate this book to my wife Katia, and my kids Danny, Sonia, Claudia and Anthony, who put up with my incessant questioning of apparently mundane things and simple objects, not knowing for years that I was simply solidifying my beliefs in what I knew I will eventually have to put in words.

To my wife and kids, and to all human kind I say: Although not intended as such, and not purposely aimed at any one group, religion, belief or faith, I have no illusions that these writings will undoubtedly seem to demystify some beliefs, debunk some theories, and otherwise appear to say that everyone else is wrong and I am correct in my interpretation of how God exists and how he meant for this universe to function. And I am perfectly aware that somewhere, in some place, there will be someone, or some group who would not hesitate to do me harm in order to silence me and to stop me from propagating my thoughts and beliefs. To those and all I say that if I let these concerns dissuade me from writing and publishing the "Truth", I would have played in their hands, and executed their plan. They would have won.

I am simply writing to tell the "TRUTH".

The "Truth" is there, it has to be told, someone has to take the initiative to tell it, even at the risk to their well-being. If I don't tell it because I am concerned about what may happen to me, who will tell it? Certainly it will not be told by those who I am concerned with, namely the religious leaders. They are too concerned with maintaining the status quo in order to preserve their hold on whatever powers and status they have achieved. They have done this by scaring their followers into unfounded sets of belief systems that for the most part put people down and make them believe in their hearts and minds that they are of a lesser quality than their God intended them to be. These so-called leaders, with very few and rare exceptions, are too coward to retract the falsehoods they learned from their predecessors, and that they are too willing and happy to propagate.

They may try, and perhaps they may succeed in silencing me in the end. As I will point out later in this book, I, or any one of us, by ourselves are not too important. But taken collectively, we have an unimaginable amount of power to speak that no one can suppress. Try as they may, they will not deter me, or anyone else from speaking the truth.

My guiding principles are very simple:

Say the truth and walk away. Let it defend itself.

Say the truth and walk away. It will beckon truth seekers from every corner of the world.

Say the truth and walk away. It will spark new ways of thinking in people who have never uttered a word in its defense, or dared to formulate a thought about it for fear of persecution, even though they always knew it in their hearts.

Say the truth and walk away. You will never change anyone's mind by hanging around an debating it for ever. They have to sort things out for themselves. In the end, dark hearts and closed minds will stay that way, no matter what.

Say the truth and walk away. Not in a retreating manner, but rather in matter-of-fact sort of way, similar to a wise man giving advice in the town's square. He does not hang around to force people to heed his advice, or to argue with them the merits of learning from their ancestors' experience. He is wise because he leaves it up to them to take the action that best suits their needs. Invariably, there will be those who do not listen, those who listen but do nothing, and those whose hearts vibrate in resonance with the spoken words. They are the ones who will perpetuate the goodness of mankind's experience.

Say the truth and walk away. God did the same thing. He created the whole universe with the intention of not walking away in an abandoning way, but in the same all-loving way a parent lets go of their child and watches the wonderful things the child can accomplish with the gifts the parent gave him; life and its lessons.

With the complete, undaunted, and clear faith and belief in what God bestowed on me, I write this book.

Let the truth be told. Let no one stop it from being told. I am deeply humbled that I was given the gift to even think that I am the one who should tell it.

So help me God.

1

Why are we here?

One day in the spring of 1998, and after our family finished lunch with our friends, we just sat around the kitchen table sipping Turkish coffee and sampling desserts. I asked my friend this simple question: Why are we here, on this earth? What is the purpose of all this? And to what end?

Perhaps a bit of background is needed first. I have known and lived with my friend since 1968. We spent four years in college where we were dorm mates, four years at the airlines working on the same airplanes in the same hangar, then as immigrants to the USA flying on the same air plane, and were roommates until we both got married in 1981 and each started raising a family.

We worked for the same aircraft manufacturer for 23 years until I moved to Texas. In few words, and until each of us started raising his family, we spent more time together than with our own siblings and extended families.

It is safe to say that each of us got to know how the other thinks. Many times we would finish each other's sentences.

So in a way, I did not have to preamble my question, or go through elaborate topic setting for my friend to understand exactly what I was asking about. He knew immediately that my question was not only philosophical in nature, but rather pertaining to practical issues facing all of us human beings and how we relate first to our Creator and second, to one another.

With this intimate insight into my way of thinking, my friend answered, without hesitation: We are here to Glorify Him.

None of us human beings are born with a religious preference; Religion is, for a lot of us, a whole lot of us, imposed on us by the family and the environment we are born in.

I was born into a Christian family, so I was raised as a Catholic. My Friend was born in a Druze family, so naturally he was raised as a Druze. Druze is a sect of Islam with the main tenet being a belief in reincarnation, and a much less emphasis on daily prayers routine and other outwardly exhibits of religiousness than most religions I am familiar with. However, a Druze does believe in God and calls him Allah. He also believes in the predetermination of spans of lives and all events, planned and accidental. In this regard, the Druze share the same basic belief with the other major religions such as Christianity and Islam, that God has predetermined EVERYTHING from start to finish. So practically, in these sets of beliefs, there are no accidental events in this world. They appear accidental to us, but they are all predetermined by God.

And OUR purpose on this earth or in this universe is to execute the PLAN of God.

So naturally, and being the ever inquisitive type that I am, I asked my friend, in an obvious and matter-of-fact way, the logical next questions:

IF GOD HAS MADE ALL THINGS AND KNOWS WHAT WILL HAPPEN AT EVERY INSTANCE, THEN WHY DOES HE NEED US? MORE IMPORTANTLY, WHY DOES HE NEED US TO "GLORIFY" HIM? AND WHY DID HE GIVE US THE POWER OF REASONING AND QUESTIONING IF ALL WE ARE DOING IS EXECUTING A PREDETREMINED PLAN, LIKE A ROBOT COMMANDED BY ITS PROGRAMMER?

I am certain that no single individual or group knows exactly who or what God is, or his purpose for our existence. Many, many things about our conception of God, just do not add up, and will not stand in the face of Logic and Reason. Perhaps they stand the test of faith, simply because faith needs no proof or logic or reason. It is just faith, and whatever someone elects to believe in becomes their reality and proof, no need for logic here.

I may have put doubt in my friend's mind about my deep belief in the existence of God, and I am not in the least concerned that he has looked at me or thought of me in any lesser way than he ever did because he may now think that I am a heretic. Not the least bit. On the contrary, I am certain that he has developed a greater appreciation for my inquisitive nature, which he knew I had from the day we met back in college.

As most Lebanese conversations tend to meander around and about, and since we both had kids who wanted to disband after lunch and wives who wanted to discuss other matters, we never got the chance to really put the finishing touches on our discussion. We, like most of us human beings, got busy with our lives . . . .

However, from that moment on, I do not recall a day where I did not think, for at least a fleeting moment, about where our thoughts would have taken us, if we were given the chance to continue our discussions.

I have since become an observer of myself, of other people, of the natural world with all its wonders, and I have become an even more persistent questioner of the intricate and absolutely amazing creation I call "The human experiment".

It is about it that I have been engaged in what some people might consider as blasphemy, others might consider as denial of the existence of Go, others might consider as though I have completely lost all touch with reality and have gone mad. The fact is that it has consumed me totally and completely.

There comes a point for all of us, after an idea has been brewing in our minds and hearts, where we have to shout it out. Most of us are either too timid to believe that we are on to something big, or too scared to speak about it, either for fear of being ridiculed (And this happened to some of the brightest minds in history), or being accused of wanting to buck the trends and destroy well-established ideas and belief systems. The sad part is that we stop there and ignore the fact that all ideas and belief systems were started by people like us. Not only this, but they too replaced other ideas and belief systems. And some of those people, at least one that I know of, was not only ridiculed, but also crucified and put to death, Jesus Christ. Others were jailed and killed; think of Ghandi and Martin Luther King. Others, not yet born and no one knows what new ideas and new belief systems they will think of, will surely have their share of detractors and persecutors. But just like others that preceded them, (Humanity is never at a loss of courageous thinkers), they too will find the courage and conviction of their righteousness to shout out loud and speak the truth.

It has only taken me since that spring day in 1998 to summon the courage and carve out the required time to put my thoughts on paper. I am a procrastinator by nature. I don't like it a bit, but that is who I am. I recognize it, and I work with whatever God gave me. People who do not understand this, have no idea how hard it is for procrastinators to just sit down and get busy, let alone finish what they have started.

So here I go.

2

Some universal truths.

Let us take a simple case of identifying the constituents of a very basic an abundant matter on earth, water. We all have come to accept, without any questioning or doubt that water is made up of two elements, hydrogen and oxygen. Through scientific experimentation and analysis, we have come to understand water's properties, its behavior under various conditions, and manipulated it to suit our purposes.

Now let us entertain the following: Would it have made any difference how we use water if scientists had gave it another name? Or called its constituents different names? Or if we have decided that its freezing and boiling temperatures are set at other than what we commonly use today? The answer is certainly NOT. Water is water, and will behave according to the laws of physics, without deviation.

The point I am trying to make is that there are universal truths about everything in this universe. And regardless of what labels we attach to them, they will always be what they are and what they were intended to do.

Just because in the Celsius scale water freezes at 0 degree, and boils at 100 degrees, and in the Fahrenheit scale it freezes at 32 degrees and boils at 212 degrees, does not make one or the other scales more right or wrong. Both scales interpret the same behavior, albeit via different routes, but they convey the same results. Boiling water, under either scale, will still harden an egg, scold our skin, and provide steam to move a locomotive. What matters here is that we have put water to the scientific inquiry and extracted its properties in a way that allows us to "Predict" the outcome of external forces on it, but more importantly, these outcomes are always the same as long as all other conditions remain unchanged.

If we wake up tomorrow and find out that boiling an egg for over seven minutes does not yield the "Predictable" result of the egg becoming hard, wouldn't we investigate the reason for this unusual behavior? We may, for instance, find out that we are trying to boil the egg on top of Mount Everest, where water boils at a much lower temperature, thus never reaching the required boiling point. Mountain climbers found this out many years ago, the hard way.

There is ONE and ONLY ONE truth about water and its properties, whether we have called it wood, iron, oil or any other name. I will go further to state that, even if a new experiment shows us tomorrow that there is a third element in water besides hydrogen and oxygen, will not change its properties or its behavior. It will only open new uses for water that were not thought of before, no more, and no less.

This applies to ALL things in this universe, no matter what. If we start with the assumption that God created all things (Which I firmly believe in), he would not have disassociated himself from his creations, and thus have stopped being subject to the same universal truth about his interaction with all things he created. Therefore, just as there is only ONE truth about the universe and all things in it, it has to follow that there is ONE and ONLY ONE truth about God, no matter what. Whether we called him Father, Allah, Yahweh, or any other name, God is God, and he is ONE. Not only that he is one by himself, he is one with the universe. For to be disassociated from the universe, is completely uncharacteristic of a Creator. It would be as if Michael Angelo had disassociated himself from the Sistine chapel paintings the minute he finished his work.

3

The fallacies in religious teachings about God.

Let us start by this simple proposition, that there is only one God. And ask a simple question about which religion identifies him best, claims to have more access to him, and follows his commands.

The fact that there ae so many religions, with so many different ways of relating to God, tells us that either all of them are wrong, or ONLY one of them is right. You may think the following statement is absurd, but it is also a true statement that all of the religions (At least those who acknowledge the existence of a God) maybe right.

Just like in the case of water, different groups may have arrived at understanding the constituents of water, and given them different names, and ultimately they all understood water's behavior and put it to their use, the case for God must follow the same rationale. God is God, no matter what.

The problem with religions is that they all have appointed themselves the missionaries of God, and some of them claim that God had spoken, literally, to their Prophets, and given them the uncontested right to steer their followers one way or another.

Another question can be posed here: Why would God want to speak to one of his people and not to another, or everyone? Why would God need to speak to his people at all? If he had created them with enough intelligence and with the power of reason and deduction, surely they should be able to infer God's wishes and his commands.

What made God wait until about the last few thousand years of mankind's existence to reveal himself? Was this intended to punish the millions of generations before? Or did he not believe they will understand? More importantly than these questions is the observation that, since we existed on this earth, and perhaps in this universe, we have proven that we are a strong bunch, and could survive, "presumably" without any divine intervention in our daily lives, for millions of years and under much less ideal conditions than those prevailing since the advent of religion.

The truth is we were never left alone, but we were given free and unfettered freedom to be ourselves, and by doing so, have proven beyond a shadow of a doubt that we are God's creations, all of us, no exceptions.

It is the height of hypocrisy for religious people to claim that they know the ways of God more or better than anyone of us. Their problem is that they have taken themselves too seriously about their role in our lives, and in a very intrusive and much maligned manner. And by doing so, they have bestowed on themselves undeserved, unwelcome, and utterly unwanted holy powers. For some of them, the blame is not theirs. It falls squarely on the shoulders of their higher-ups who for one reason or another have manipulated everyone into believing that they and they alone, know the TRUTH.

I have a sneaky suspicion, and almost a certainty that all of this is driven by the desire to have power. Power is the ultimate aphrodisiac, it corrupts, and it certainly has corrupted the religious "leaders". I have to apologize for calling them Leaders; a more apt name would be "Manipulators". They are not to blame; the blame falls on all of us, for neglecting the fact that we are ALL children of the same God, who would be eternally dismayed with us for acting in a manner that contradicts the powers conferred on us the instant we were born.

Another important issue I need to raise at this point revolves around the sheer number of religions. If there is only one God, why then are there so many religions? Unless we take the hypothesis that there are as many Gods as religions today, and this will automatically lead us to believe that many more Gods will be "Invented" as many new religions get invented in the future.

If we believe, as the majority of modern religions believe, that there is only one God, the question becomes: Which religion has it right? Surely they are not all wrong, and just as surely they are not all right, since we have demonstrated earlier that there will always be ONE TRUTH about anything and everything in this universe, and no matter how we describe or call anything or being, will not change what, or who it is.

Assuming all modern religions believe in the same God, why then does each religion accord itself a proprietary method of worship and practices aimed at communicating with God? And here I am not at all advocating the absolute need for worship, just that these religions have established the "Want" for worship.

What is so strikingly strange to me about most religious practices is their hypocrisy in claiming that they worship God for God's glory, when most of their prayers involve asking favors from God: Protect us, guide us, sanctify us, and keep us from evil, so forth and so on. It almost sounds and looks and feels like they are political lobbyists currying favors with God, but disguising their requests in prayers and words and acts of glorification. If they truly believe in one omnipotent and loving God, these practices are absolutely not needed. The fact that they believe in the necessity for these practices indicates that they either are not sure God knows what we need (Or want), or perhaps they want to make sure that God listen to their prayers and not the others. Both of these reasons are false and contradictory to our concept of God. It is as if a child feels the need to glorify and pray to its mother so she feeds it and protects it from harm. Here, let us not confuse a baby crying when it is hungry with adults currying favors. God has created us with instinctive behaviors when we are born that far surpass any reasoning power we may acquire as we get older. These behaviors are "Natural", untainted by collateral desires and wants, and in and by themselves are material proof of God's unlimited wisdom and ultimate perfection in his creations.

4

Why, then, did we all accept Religion?

My guess is that, whether we like it or not, we are all born with different degrees of intelligence and unequal powers of reasoning and deduction. However, this does not make any of us more or less valuable as a human being. It just means that the way our brains are arranged, and the way they process information, are different from one person to the other. It is just a matter of pure genetic make-up, with perhaps some degree of influence from the environment we are born and raised in, and the access to varying levels of education. More importantly, it is influenced to the greatest degree by the presumed freedom to question, inquire, and arrive at certain conclusions. If one society forbids or suppresses the freedom of thought and outward expression, it will put a damper on the most inquisitive minds. Alternatively, if society allows these freedoms and encourages them, it will draw the most out of even the simplest minds.

Two famous astronomers once discovered that indeed the earth is not at the center of the universe, and proclaimed it publicly. We all know that they were publicly ridiculed by the Christian church and its leaders, and one was put under house arrest. The church did not have any scientific basis for their claims that the earth was at the center of the universe, but since this belief was at the core of their teachings and the source of their power, it had no choice but to act the way it did. I assert that had Copernicus and Galileo discovered this fact few hundred years before or after, none of this would have happened. On the contrary, they would have been celebrated and maybe given the Nobel prize for scientific discovery.

Religions did not invent God; God existed in the minds of human beings for millennia before any religion was even thought of. Even early man aspired to a higher power and had some inkling about the existence of a power far beyond his comprehension, and expressed these beliefs in his primitive way, nonetheless just as pure and unadulterated as a newborn who is raised in complete isolation from our teachings about God.

It is for the lack of higher thought power in the majority of human beings that we have all accepted religion and its teachings about God. Perhaps in the beginning religious people had good intentions by steering all of us one way or another, however and as soon as religious leaders discovered what a powerful tool religion truly is, they got corrupted by their own invention and became addicted to it, even if it meant inventing things about God that had no proof and no basis, except their desire to keep us all "in line".

This by no mean is meant to allude that religion is a bad thing. On the contrary, absolute religion and the eventual absolute faith in the existence of God are two of the most brilliant deductions we, as human beings, have come up with, ever. How we used them has been a complete and absolute travesty of the universal truth about God and his purpose for us being on this earth.

By the way, and until someone presents evidence to the contrary, we are the only human species God created, there are no other human beings on any other planet. Period. I will elaborate on this point later on in this book. Suffice it to say at this point that it does not make any sense for God to have created human beings on any other planet besides earth. I would not have done so. Would you? If you were God? And to what end or purpose?

5

What would you do if YOU were God?

Let us take the simple hypothesis that in the beginning there was nothing; which most religious and non-religious people would probably agree upon, since we have no physical and irrefutable evidence that planet earth, or the universe at large, were populated in the beginning of time. So no one could bear witness to the contrary.

So, the setting of the universe would be such as there was only matter, animate or inanimate is immaterial, and perhaps the animals existed then, since they are not the topic o this assumption, being just as perfect as everything else, since they were created by God, the most perfect being of all.

In a setting were everything is "Perfect", there is "Stagnation". By definition, a perfect thing, or being, cannot evolve or change to a higher (or lower) degree of state, since it is "Perfect". We can

16

marvel ONLY for so long at a painting by Picasso or Da Vinci, or the most advanced technological product of our times, even if it performed amazing operations. In the end, and after a short while, WE, human beings, get restless with it, and bored with the repetition of whatever feelings it exhorted from us or tasks it generated, and we demand a higher state of "Perfection". This in fact, negates the definition of perfection we assign to anything.

Perfection becomes "Boring" immediately at the instance following our being amazed by it. And we are the "Imperfect" beings. How would God feel if he had created the universe and everything in it in a perfect state?

I am not advocating that the first human beings would have reasoned in this manner, being preoccupied with their own survival and not having yet witnessed the amazing power of their own race to demonstrate their unique capabilities, as compared to all other creatures. What I am proposing here is that, in the absence of a rock-solid proof otherwise, God created us, human beings, to indeed "Glorify Him", as my friend suggested an believed sincerely in his heart, albeit not in the absolute meaning of the word "Glorify", and certainly not through prayers, acts of contrition, religious practices, and absolutely not through conveying on God our own human titles and attributes. God simply dos not need or want us to do any of these things. He simply wants us to "Amaze" him with our ingenuity and inventiveness.

How did we accomplish amazing things, and still are working hard to accomplish even more amazing things in the eyes and mind of God?

We did it all, and will keep on doing it because God created us with one beautiful gift he did not give to any other of his creations: IMPERFECTION.

A simple observation of how the animals and plants and all other living things live and survive is solid proof that they are as perfect as can be. They do not need shelter, or clothing, or a feeling of belonging to a social network in order to perpetuate their species. They act in unison with the non-human universe in a harmonious way where they all serve a dual role, feed themselves and be food for others. The old saying that animals live to eat and humans eat in order to live is a perfect way to describe the non-human universe as a perfectly tuned machine that does not need any intervention from outside sources, or ingenuity from within itself to exist and prosper.

Us human beings, on the other hand, were created with this "Imperfection", of needing to extract from our surroundings elements that do not occur naturally, but rather require a high degree of thought and processing to fulfill needs we know we have; But more importantly to fulfill desires we did not know we had until we discovered that there are ways to achieve even higher and higher degrees of satisfaction, just by applying our innate thought processes.

Primitive man, assuming there was really one man and one woman in the beginning (A theory that is completely and utterly devoid of any sound reasoning and logic) could not have survived and populated the earth. The physical odds are against such a theory. Setting aside the onslaught of the elements such as extreme cold and hot temperatures, not to mention the numerous predators, it is highly conceivable that Adam and Eve could have had as children either only boys or only girls. Then what? How could they have populated the earth?

There is nothing wrong with the multitude of religious and other secular theories about the creation of man and setting his race apart from all other creations. These theories serve a very tangible purpose in simplifying the whole process to the average human being. However, when the "Custodians" of these beliefs and theories stepped outside the immediate purpose of assuring that we all accept certain things as fact (In spite of the fact to the contrary), they began to promulgate other and non-related beliefs and conjectures that deviated from the initial purpose, and thus set the stage for other "Theories" that are just as deviant and destructive to the human mind and its creative powers.

When you take a new-born and start pumping in his brain your own falsehoods about where he came from and the purpose of him being on this earth for many years, and you reinforce these falsehoods with a system of rewards and punishments that are absolutely and completely baseless in the eyes of God, you will have effectively thwarted his ability to use his God-given free will and awesome power of deduction to really GLORIFY his Creator, God.

We see this in abundant evidence in under-developed societies, where the sheer human desire and drive to survive in extreme conditions have led to the majority of these societies subscribing to a set of beliefs and practices that are naturally in complete contradiction to what these majorities would have adopted under more logical and practical set of conditions.

Let us take the simple case of the United States of America. This is a country made up of mostly non-native people, who have come from almost every other country on earth. Yet, the

USA does not resemble any one of these varied countries, not in constitution, not in spirit, not in religion, not in civil law, not in anything that the origin countries believe in, either in specific rules or practices. The American people, within the guidelines of their constitutional freedoms, set a system of basic human freedoms of thought and act (Within the guidelines of their constitutional freedoms) that has few elements from the origin countries imbedded in it. (The founding fathers had to start by either adopting the good practices or new ones that remedied the shortcomings of the bad ones). And within this system, there are so many rules and practices that are specifically and succinctly aimed at not falling in the corrupt trap of practices originating in either the origin countries or have been imported and twisted by their importers to further their cause and their hold on power over other people.

I am in no way claiming that the American system is the pinnacle of perfection, I am simply making an observation that those same human beings that were born and raised in other societies and systems, have collectively decided that their homelands did not provide them with the TRUE human environments to excel in, and that their interests are best served by adopting new rules and practices that will foster an environment where they, individually and collectively, can live with, but more importantly can prosper in.

Could the native Indian–American have achieved the same? Perhaps yes, but I submit that the answer is a strong maybe, leaning towards the NO. Not because I don't believe that the Native Indians have less brain power that the settlers, but rather because they ad no other frame of reference to go by. Someone who flees his country because he was persecuted for his religious beliefs will surely want to set up a system in his newly adopted country that is tolerant of all religions. The Indians did not have that bad experience, therefore they would not have seen the need to even address the issue. Someone who flees his country because only a handful of people can hold political offices and become governors of the people will surely want to set a democratic political system in his newly adopted country. The Indians, to our knowledge, did not bother with politics and public offices, so they had no need to even address the issue.

The simple fact that the Indians have lived and survived, and more importantly they prospered for thousands of years before any white man have set foot on the continent, is proof positive that they have equal, if not greater intellect and understanding of their world than the white race.

I have digressed a bit, but I wanted to make a point, without looking as if I am slighting one race in favor of another. The point I was making is that, thru the very young American experiment, we have proof positive that human beings, given the absolute freedom to chose, will always gravitate towards their Godly nature, which loves liberty (Of body and spirit,) progress, advancement, and the glorification of God through a continuous improvement of the human condition, and not through the empowerment of one man over another or one nation over others.

In the game of power that has been played for millennia by the various nations and empire and kingdoms, there always have been losers. These losers were not only those who lost the physical act of war, but to a large degree the presumed winners were also losers of sorts. Perhaps not in the immediate period after the war has ended, but definitely in the long run.

History has shown that no nation can govern another nation, for ever. Perhaps for a long time, tens and maybe hundreds of years, but eventually the native people will always overcome their occupiers, one way or another. Yet, nations still wage wars, chasing the ever elusive dream of being the conquerors. And what has been the one common price paid by humanity for all these wars? Death and destruction on all sides.

Many of the wars waged by most civilizations were waged under the misguided cause of religion, therefore of God. We have all seen their foolishness, and experienced their atrocities. So, let no one try to attempt at convincing us that these nations and their leaders really understood the concept of God. Far from it, they only used God and religion to mask the real intent behind their actions: POWER and DOMINANCE.

No one wants power for power's sake. Surely some of us, maybe a lot of us, enjoy power and what it gives us in unquantifiable pleasures, but these pleasures are short-lived and ultimately we will always seek higher levels of power to obtain higher (Or different) levels of pleasure. And since there is a limited amount of pleasure derived from a pure of sense of power over others, there has to be another more tangible reason as to why we tend to fight. This other reason is unequivocally materialistic in nature, whether it is real estate, wealth, money, and a host of other material possessions. However, the most common reason why nations fought throughout history is: Land and its riches. And since we all know that there is a very limited and non-renewable amount of land and natural resources there will always be wars. And here are the biggest and most simple arguments for the existence of one God and for our being his ONLY creations in the universe.

To begin with, let us ask the question: Why would God create only one universe, and yet create two Peoples? We have demonstrated, as laid out above, and as we have witnessed throughout history that WE will fight over whatever exists in our world. Therefore, should there be another People somewhere else in this universe, it follows logically that we will fight over whatever exists in the whole universe, no matter how big this universe is or ho much we are convinced it contains resources in enough abundance for all of us.

If we assume that God created another People on another planet, then logic tells us that he may have also created a third, perhaps a fourth, or maybe an unlimited number of Peoples. Why not? I will lay out the rationale why not.

We learn in our early childhood that, no matter how big a pie is, it gets smaller the instance it gets divided; not only in half, but in many other pieces. Therefore, no matter how big and huge and expansive this universe is, it becomes limited and indeed starts getting smaller the minute it gets divided between not only two Peoples, but perhaps over many, many more. I do not want to even imagine what will happen between these Peoples once they each discover that they have to share with others.

It makes absolutely no sense for God to have created us on this Earth, only to see us fight with others over a divided universe. We certainly do enough fighting on this Earth for the **presumably** limited resources. I say presumably limited, because an all-loving God would not have created us and has a higher and nobler purpose for us, only to see us perish because there are insufficient resources to see us through, for eternity. This fabricated state of limited resources was created because some groups want more of the pie than the others, and are willing to sacrifice God's children in their pursuit to acquire more for themselves.

The ONLY way God would have set up this whole universe is to have one and ONLY one species like ourselves, perpetually evolving and progressing towards higher and higher states of perfection. Does this mean that we are all doing the right thing? Or behaving in a way that pleases God? Not necessarily. For the God that created the human race to be in his image and accomplish unexpected and amazing things, has also endowed it with the freedom of CHOICE. This freedom is absolute and cannot be restricted in one way or another. Should there be restrictions of our freedom to act in a completely unpredicted way, is tantamount to having God create us in a "Perfect" condition, and thus negating the very powerful force of "Invention" that is the result of us being "Imperfect".

PERFECTION IS BORING AND STAGNANT.
IMPERFECT BEINGS HAVE THE POWER
AND DESIRE TO ACHIEVE.
GOD WOULD NOT HAVE CREATED
US IN ANY OTHER WAY.
GOD DOES NOT LOVE STAGNATION.
GOD LOVES THE PURSUIT OF PERFECTION,
EVEN IF IT BRINGS WITH IT IMPERFECT
ACTS FROM IMPERFECT BEINGS.

6

The most difficult, yet the ONLY and logical decision: What would you have done if you were GOD?

For those of us, and we are the majority, who believe that in the beginning there was nothing, and only God existed, I pose this question: What was he the God of? Was he the God of nothing? It is utterly inconceivable to even think that God would have presided over void. It would be like a king without a kingdom.

For this simple reason (And I am certain there are more reasons) I say that there were never nothing in this universe, there never was a complete void, all material things existed, not from the "Start" as we define the start of all things, but before the start and even before that.

I do not want to take any religion's side on this issue, but merely assert that some religions, especially those who believe that God has no beginning and no end, may have reasoned or stumbled over the same conclusion, that God had no beginning, no present and no end. God simply "Is", "Has always been" and "Will always be". Period.

There simply cannot be any other explanation, for to explain it in any other worldly, physical, mathematical, chemical or any other way will imply limitations on the nature of God that are contradictory to his qualities by putting bounds on his being, knowledge, power, and more importantly on his timeline. God has no timeline, since he had no beginning and will have no end.

If we, for the moment, come to accept the proposition laid out above, that God simply exists, and all material things existed with him from the get-go, then the question I posed in the opening of these writings becomes a very natural question to ask? Why are we here? Was God not satisfied with the Universe and all things he had created that he saw the need to create yet one more? And I assert that this is the one LAST creation he created. Knowing all things, and knowing full well that if he is to create Man, with all the talents and shortcomings of human nature, especially the one shortcoming dealing with bad thoughts, deeds, feelings, criminal acts against other human beings and all God's creatures, God decided that, after all it is far better to create Man than to keep the Universe as it was in perfect balance and eternal harmony.

However, what good would it do anyone if God had created Man as just anther of his other "Perfect" creations? There can be absolutely no reason to add another "Perfect" creature to the already existing "Perfect" ones. This new creature will melt in this pot of Creations and will not be distinguishable from any other. On the other hand, and in order to have a dynamic Universe, one that will constantly surprise, amaze, delight, and yes indeed Glorify God, Man had to be created in an "Imperfect" condition, albeit with an innate thought processing power and inquisitiveness that no other creature has, or will ever have.

It never ceases to amaze me how no thinker, no philosopher, no preacher, and no prophet has ever articulated these same deductions in words. My hunch is that those early "Preachers" and men of God, who were indeed very smart and highly in tune with the Universe, either did not believe that their fellow men will understand their true nature, or they figured that by keeping the truth to themselves and feeding their peoples their own message, they will gather more power and have more authority over everyone; and why not? Did they not speak in the name of God?

I am fully aware of the dilemmas these early Preachers were facing. On one hand, people had no spiritual guidance and no moral compass, and someone needed to lay down the law in order to have some civility. This someone could not, or would not propose any guidance emanating from a human being; he had to attribute the guidance to a higher power, lest the people would ridicule him and reject his message. Why would any human being follow another human being? People are more inclined to follow someone if he portrays his message as being from a higher power, like God.

It is very simple to put this to the test, now just as well as millions of years ago or millions of years in the future. Have an employee of a company go and tell his fellow workers that he thinks a new rule should be implemented, because he had thought about it an decided, rather concluded that this new rule is for the better of everyone. What are the chances he will succeed?

However, the same employee, announcing that upper management has issued the same rule (Even without any explanation or elaborate rationale), will have a much higher probability of other workers accepting the new rule; How can they not accept a new rule dictated by a higher power, UPPER MANAGEMENT.

So there it happened, thousands of years ago, that some smart (And perhaps well-intentioned) bunch of men figured out a way to corral the rest of the herd and have them believing in their own version of God, and therefore steering them into a more civilized behavior towards one another, at least on the average. There were always holdouts, and there will always be holdouts. These individuals, for one reason or another, either saw through all the smoke or were just intent on being dissenters for the fun of it. Either way, even among the same flock, there were always, and will always be those presumed believers who will always defy the rule of the law, or religion. What is amazing to me is that invariably bad things did not happen to these dissenters at any lower or higher rates than others that are presumed to be believers and true followers of the "RULE".

So what happened to the rule or belief that those who disregard "God's" rule or commit acts of behavior that are not good in the eyes of God will be punished and forever banished from the promised eternal life?

Let us begin by asking some very obvious questions, to which we were never given the obvious answers.

Why would God favor one of his creatures over the rest, and entrust in him or her with the delivery of his message to the rest of us? Why would God not speak to us all, like having an all-hands meeting once in a while? Why should we be more inclined to believe in the message if it were delivered by a "Messenger" from God rather from God himself? Would we not feel slighted if our parents spoke to us via one of their kids, instead of speaking to all of us or to each one of us directly? I would. Not only that I would feel slighted, but I would feel that I am a lesser child in the eyes of my parents, and I would certainly be driven to behaving in manners that not congruent with whatever "Normal" and "Predicted" behavior they expected of me. And surely, some of this behavior will not be judged as "Good" behavior, and I may get punished for it.

To all my fellow human beings I say, the whole thing is much simpler than portrayed throughout the ages, yet can be very daunting to explain due to the sheer size and complexity of this universe and how incomprehensible to our human brains it is to fathom such a universe being "Simple".

God created us all in his image and as his representatives on Earth, and he did not create us to keep "Tinkering" with us. He wanted us to be spitting images of him, albeit not exactly like him. We were created in an imperfect condition, but that is exactly where the beauty of all this lies

7

How it all came into being.

After God has finished his creations of the universe, with its planets and stars and galaxies, and after he had created a special place for living things and called it Earth, he marveled at how beautiful everything was that he had created. More importantly, God marveled at how harmonious the universe was, and how even the simplest of all his creatures, behaved in a perfect way.

Planets revolved in predetermined orbits, stars died and stars were born, galaxies swallowed other galaxies, but the whole system functioned in a perfect and predictable manner.

Vegetations grew, blossomed, bore fruits and seeds to regenerate their species, withered and died, but their seeds came into life and restarted the whole process once again, and again, for all eternity.

The animal kingdom offered the most dazzling display of perfection. Without any intervention from outside, they followed their Godly instinct and became predators and preys, but nevertheless they executed the Godly plan to perfection.

Tiny and helpless new-born were provided with their mothers' protection and food so they could reach maturity, all this in spite of their living in the midst of untold numbers of dangers and predators. They stayed close to their mothers and learned survival skills and became adults and lived the rest of their lives in their perfect world.

Everything worked in perfect harmony, and everything pleased God with his work.

But . . . .

Even though anyone would marvel at how wonderful the universe worked to perfection, there was something missing indeed: Creativity.

Surely some plants developed highly advance tactics to deal with their environment and changed some of their innate characteristics in order to survive and prosper. Surely most animals, even those we consider unchanged for millions of years, evolved in countless ways to adapt to their surroundings.

But none of all God's creations before Man "Changed" the world around it, and used its brain power to overcome its natural deficiency that I call "Imperfection".

And without man's coming onto the scene, with all of his qualities, the good and the bad, the creative and the destructive, the faithful and the blasphemist, this universe was ever doomed to be static, stagnant, and most depressing of all, boring. And God saw that, and decided to interject one more creature that will exceed all others in its creativity, albeit this creativity had to come from a deficiency not in any other creature. Imperfection. And this will set in motion God's plan to perpetuate his eternal desire to not have to "Tinker" or "Tweak" his creation any more.

God then decided to create Man.

8

Would you have done it differently if YOU, were God?

I don't know about you and what you would do if you were faced with a momentous decision such as the one dealing with creating another being that is so close to your image, endowed with a lot of your qualities, but yet not a copy of you. And I need to admit here that it makes absolutely no sense to create Man, endow him with intelligence and with creativity, yet make him less perfect than the rest of creations, and still hang around and intervene in his affairs for ever and ever.

Parents beget children and raise them until they are self-supporting adults, capable of making their own decisions, (and yes making their own mistakes), but ultimately conquering over their deficiencies. As we all know, parents do not hang around for ever. Parents pass on and their children perpetuate their lineage, and their grandchildren after them repeat the same cycle of life. Why then would God hang around forever, in a physical sense? If it is to make sure his creations are well-taken care of, or to make sure they do not commit irreversible acts of self-destruction, or otherwise not fulfill his "grand Plan", he has defeated the purpose of creating them in the first place.

So, in his ultimate wisdom and boundless knowledge and keen insight into the future, God has made the ultimate decision: The only way to give Man the freedom to "Be", is for God to not disappear from the scene, but rather to become an observer of how his wonderful creations will fulfill his GRAND plan.

God then, seeing that there is only way for Man to be created in a Glorious manner, and inherit the world, and Glorify God, committed the ultimate act of creation and created man. He created man and in his own image and with his all his creativity. He gave him intelligence, he gave him creativity, he gave him complete freedom of thought, he gave him the ability to reproduce and propagate his race (And this last one sits in a very special place of importance among all other qualities, as I will discuss later). However, the one thing God did not ask man to do was to glorify him with words or acts of religious nature. God wanted man to glorify him by being himself, by improving himself, and ultimately by proving God was right in the first place to entrust Man with this World.

God, by performing this ultimate act, has set in motion the most amazing of his creations. This creation does not need (Or want) any intervention from any outside source. Even from the Creator himself. For to ask the creator to intervene, even it is only one time, will negate the beautiful purpose for setting Man free, absolutely free. I submit to you that God, by setting things up in this manner, has assured the perpetuity of all things, including himself. As we said before, that there can be no king without a kingdom and it subjects, there also cannot be a God without his Creations, and specifically without his ultimate Creation, Mankind.

It is not too difficult, even for the simplest mind, to put all this in the right perspective, if one can free their mind from the chatter of religious teachings and all the other corrupt concepts about God and our relationship with him.

If only we start by asking the same simple question I asked my friend in the opening of these writings, why are we here? Then a series of logical deductions will lead any normal person to the same and only conclusion:, and my friend was right: We are here to Glorify God.

Every time we overcome a difficulty. Every time we uncover a secret of the natural world. Every time we invent new technologies, new products, and better products. Every time we come to each other's assistance, lend a helping hand to someone in need, or rescue someone in trouble.

All one has to do is look at the difference between Man and the rest of God's creatures and Creations to understand that we hold a very special place in this universe. The dinosaurs lived for millions and millions of years, and admittedly evolved physically (And perhaps a bit in their metal capacities or instincts), but eventually they became extinct, the last of them not distinguishable from the first. Not only that they did not improve themselves, but they left absolutely no mark on the world around them, lest we consider their fossils a mark. Other creatures, extinct or still evolving, having being around for millions of years more than Mankind, have not interacted with their surroundings in the same way, in the slightest bit, as we did.

This is in no way meant to make these creatures of God less deserving of being God's creations than Man. On the contrary, they are fulfilling their roles, to perfection, as prescribed by their Creator. And in doing so, they also Glorify God.

However, our role is nobler and much more complex, and all of it emanates from this very small imperfection God imbedded in us, on purpose, to spark the everlasting cycle of Humanity and its accomplishments.

9

This is why "WE" are here

Have you ever thought what would have happened to the Universe, or what would happen to it in the future, if one human being simply did not exist? Or maybe a lot of human beings did not exist or suddenly disappeared? What difference would it make to this enormous march by humanity from our early beginnings towards the ultimate end, if there is one?

My hunch says that nothing would happen that was not supposed to happen. Perhaps some events would take place in different places and at different times, but whatever was ordained to happen will eventually happen. All of us are not just the collection of each and every one of us, specifically. But we need all of us to make us who we are and what we have been destined to become and what we have been ordained to do by God.

In this infinite world we live in, there are infinite numbers of natural laws to discover, infinite numbers of individuals to discover them, as well as and infinite amount to time to do it in. Practically we have all eternity to do what we are supposed to do in the grand plan of God.

Let us look at few examples, and start by one of the most obvious discoveries, fire.

No one is absolutely certain when man stumbled upon fire and saw that it is a good thing for him and his kind. Nor it is very important for us to pinpoint the time of discovery with any certainty. Arguably, we have no set date for this discovery, if we all assume that it was a single discovery, by a single man. Even if we accept the hypothesis that it was a single event that took place thousands, maybe millions of years ago, it would not have made any difference if it had happened one thousand years before or after the exact date. I will go further to say that it would not have made any difference if it had happened a million years either way. The main point is that, with enough people around, and with enough opportunities for a chance discovery by early man (Later discoveries are a mixture of chance and deliberate search) the discovery of fire was an event schedule to happen, albeit not on any exact timescale and not in any predetermined location or locations. Again, I need to remind the reader that for God to have scheduled this event, and all other events in our lives, would make us less than human, and more like robots and machines that are preprogrammed to execute a set plan. How wasteful would that have been?

Arguably, most discoveries made by early man were accidental in nature, however it took an enormous amount of keen observation from early man, over many generations, to understand what he was witnessing, but more importantly to deduce that certain phenomena and natural laws can be put to use for his benefit.

Later discoveries, as mentioned earlier, were more and more the result of a deliberate search for answers to questions, solutions to problems, and at the later stages, as in the 20th and 21st centuries and beyond, solution to problems that did not exist. But we figured out a way to extract highly advanced usages from the world around us, even though we did not have a problem to solve as such. We invented new technologies and new things simply because we could.

Did man need airplanes to survive and prosper? No. But man figured out that he can put certain material together and make a flying object out of them. Surely the Wright brothers did not set out to make transatlantic flight feasible, and very comfortable for millions of people. They simply wanted to demonstrate that a flying machine could be built. And they did. Only later on, after we got bored with the initial invention (No matter how perfect the Wrights saw their aircraft in their minds, and no matter how people marveled at the Wrights feat at the time), that other inventors started tinkering with the basic concept, and through trial and error, found the multitude of uses for it, albeit some of these uses were for sinister and destructive purposes. Here again, all things come as a "Package", the good mixed in with the bad.

The question begs: Should the Wright brothers have not succeeded in their attempts, would we have not discovered flight and airplanes at a later date? Surely we would have. There are many people who believe that the Wrights were not the first to do so, that there were other inventors in Europe and the Middle East and Africa who were on the same path. It makes no difference who got to it first, my point is that there are enough of us around, with inquisitive minds, to discover all that has to be discovered.

Did man need cell phones to survive and prosper? No. But man figured out that he could make electrons behave in a certain way where he can, from the comfort of his living room or deep in the Amazon jungle, press few buttons and immediately reach another person clear across the globe.

The same questions can be asked here, about almost any invention we made throughout history, and those we are yet to make in the future.

I am in no way proposing that we should abolish these inventions or go back to living primitive lives. On the contrary, I am simply citing very few examples to illustrate the "Inevitability" of all these events, simply due to our sheer numbers, but more importantly due to our inquisitiveness and innate desire to compensate for our imperfection with more and more complex inventions to make our lives better and better.

Here I need to reiterate that WE exist not as a collection of individuals that make up a group, or groups of people, but rather as a group of people that happened to be made up of individuals. Let me explain the subtle differences between the two concepts, as it relates to God and Man. As I proposed earlier, it is very inconceivable that God made one man and one woman and entrusted them to populate the earth. So naturally, and in order to set man and woman "Free" to be, and to behave, God had to create groups of people in different and remote parts of earth. How else can we explain the huge differences between the races, in the face structure, in stature, in the color of the skin, in the type of hair, and a myriad other physical differences? Note here that I do not believe in the existence of differences in our mental capabilities; these are the same in all races, or else the lesser intelligence races would not have survived and prospered along with the more intelligent ones. Besides this fact, and for many other reasons, God would not allow himself to endow one race with more or less than any other race.

Some religions work their way around the proposition that God created Adam and Eve and they begot children and their children begot children, and these handful of people became the human race as we know it, and overcome the notion of human life spans being so short as to endanger the purpose of populating the earth, by telling us that Adam and Eve, and Abraham and Noah, and most early humans lived for hundreds of years, some living close to a thousand years. Not only that they lived and prospered, but kept on having children well into their later years. Of course if one accepts these fallacies as facts, then one can easily go from there to seeing that these few people had the correct set of circumstances to make up for the fallacy of being the only ones created by God.

Even in scientific thought, you can arrive at deductions that are absolutely absurd, if you have taken some incorrect and absurd hypothesis. In other words, if one makes up the rules, then one can apply any judgments, right or wrong, as long as these judgments "fit" the rules. This in no way implies that the basic rules are correct. It just simply means that people, in the absence of a scientific approach and a verifiable method by which they can explain this seemingly complex world, have made up their own basic rules and hypotheses, and spun very intricate stories to fit their model, and voila, we have religions explaining God to us in very childish, albeit amusing ways.

The most distressing thing of all is that we, collectively, for very logical reasons, have been swept in this hysteria, but above all we dared not contradict these fallacies for well-founded self preservation reasons.

Who in their right mind, would dare tell the religious leaders that they have it all wrong? Certainly we cannot expect their followers to contradict them. And on this point, I venture to say that the followers, even if they had any doubts in their minds and hearts, would prefer to keep the status quo, if not only for fear of being excommunicated, but for the fear of not having any other belief system that can make sense out of their lives and destinies.

All these believers need to do is to open their eyes, shed the strict and unbending rules of their group, and look at this wonderful universe we live in. Everything that has been crafted came from this earth, but nothing WE invented existed in nature in a state suitable for our use.

This is by far the ultimate accomplishment that God wanted us to achieve in his name; to validate that he has made all the right decisions about us, and to insure our perpetual success, for all eternity.

Let us now examine how mankind, and all other living things go about assuring their perpetuity. When I mention living things, I want the reader to know that included in this category are all inanimate object we have considered as not living things, inorganic non-breathing matter such as rocks and soil. For I am certain these things, as any other creation of God, are living matter that is subject to the same evolutionary laws that govern all. All you have to do is examine how mountains, made up of rock and soil, are constantly evolving in their own way, under tremendous yet unseen geologic forces, and how they come into being, rise to incredible heights and then disappear to get reborn again. The difficulty we have as human beings in understanding these concepts is that they take place at such very low rates of change, and over thousands and millions of years that, to our relatively brief life span they seem to be static and unchanging. However, science has taught us differently. Just because we cannot observe a phenomenon, or even a very small segment of its evolution, from start to finish in our own time scale, does not mean it is not taking place. It is always a matter of long-term and keen observation, reinforced by scientific methods and ever subject to logical and deductive reasoning.

In the case of a parent, knowing full well that his time on earth is very limited, the most logical way to assure the continuity and perpetuation of his family, is to have kids, perhaps a lot of kids. Once the parent has passed on, his children and their descendents for generation to come will assure that his legacy will live on. I will not go as far as to say that each family line will keep on going for ever and ever. Some family lines will eventually disappear for many logical reasons. However, given the multitude of families on earth, the chances of survival of some, or the majority of them, are not only great, but have a sure and absolute certainty about them that we cannot deny.

What would please a parent about his children more than anything else? What would make a parent go out of this life with the certainty that whatever he has created will not only survive, but will excel and keep on excelling for all eternity? And is it not true that we, as parents, have the ultimate desire to see some of our own characteristics and features propagated in our offspring? Don't we desire to be remembered, if not by our grea great grand children, but at least by our children and their children? What does it mean for us, after we are gone, for anyone to remember us? What if we die without leaving anyone behind us? Do we get remembered at all, by anyone?

It is in the obvious answers to these questions that we must find the concept of God. Not in a relationship of a servant or worshipper to his master, or in a submissive and degrading way. God would not want us to act in these ways. He created us to relate to him in the same way a child relates to his parents. In the end, it boils down to this: A child cannot exist without a parent, and a parent is domed to obsolescence without a child.

In the Jewish teachings, Moses was chosen as God's first prophet. In the Christian teachings, Jesus was chosen as the Son of God. In the Muslim teachings, Mohammed was chosen as God's last prophet.

I am fine with these concepts, but they raise so many questions we cannot ignore, not to doubt the validity of God's intentions for mankind, but to start rethinking our relationship with God in a more logical way, and in a manner that can stand the test of reason.

Why Moses?
Why Jesus?
And why Mohammed?

These were fine and upstanding men no doubt, but surely there were other men deserving of these great honors.

Why has there not been a woman prophet or messenger of God? Are they of a lesser nature?

Why not chose only one prophet? Did God think we are too thick to get his message from the first prophet?

And, accepting the fact that all these prophets had the same basic tenet that asserts the presence of God, why then did their teachings diverge so wildly? (Or at least the practices of these teachings?)

Which of these religions is the "True" one? The answer cannot be all of them, and if it is one or the other, then we have to accept the fact that the others are either wrong or we have completely misinterpreted their intent.

Why not you, and me, and every other one of us children of God? God surely has the power to ingrain in each one of us the predisposition to know him from the minute we are born, and to follow his principles throughout our lives. Why not do this, instead of having immortal beings attempt to explain it all to us, with relative success, and so many times by force, intimidation, and in certain cases under the threat to our own lives?

God created us all free, and would not have sent anyone to force us in believing in him. The moment one religion starts telling us that "IT" is the right one; it is automatically telling us that the others are wrong.

It is as simple as two candidates running for election for a public office, in their stomp speeches each one is telling us that he or she has it right, which logically means that the opponent has it wrong. They cannot be both right (And I am sure that in most instances they are both wrong), because then the election process would become meaningless and we get closer to a system of appointment rather than election. And they cannot

44

both be wrong; no politician will ever admit to it (We have to discover it later on when they sit in office for years and accomplish absolutely nothing of what they promised during their campaign).

By now, I hope you, the reader, has started to formulate your own questions and to come up with your own conclusions around the main theme of this book: Why are we here and to what end purpose?

Go on, do not be afraid to ask, not in a doubting and malicious way, but rather in an inquisitive way that God meant for you and I and every other human being to possess, and use our amazing gifts to draw our own picture of the one and only certainty in the universe:

<u>God is there, and he has dissolved himself in YOU and me and all of US so he can live in humanity for ever.</u>

If you have ever wondered how beautiful and complex this universe is, and if you could for a moment put aside all the theories about evolution and creation and everything else in between, here is a very simple way of looking at things, to convince you once and for all that there has to be a Creator, there has to be a God.

Go to the auto parts store and purchase each and every part of, say a Chevrolet. I mean for you to go and purchase not only the mechanical and electrical and electronic parts, but also the fabric of the seats and the engine oil and the fuel that goes in the tank, and the paint for the exterior. Now have the store box all these items in a crate or more and deliver to your garage. Theoretically, you have a Chevrolet in your garage. But practically, all you have are pieces that are gathered together in close proximity to each other. It is only after you have assembled these parts in their predetermined order that you have a Chevrolet which you can drive. In essence, even though you did not create any single part of this car, you are in a way the creator of it, by the mere act of assembly. We can all admit to the fact that a car, no matter how advanced, is still a very insignificant and primitive object, compared with the living things in this universe.

Now compare the relative simplicity of a car to the intricate and complex make-up of this universe, with its planets, galaxies, stars, moons, plants, animals, and of course people. Think how all these things have worked together for millions and perhaps billions of years. Think how even if these things existed in a physical sense, they would still be "Parts in a box", devoid of any meaningful action, and incapable of drawing on each other's resources to live and prosper, until they are put together, not as an assembly, but as a coherent system by their Creator, God.

As noted earlier, and accepting for the time being that God did create the universe with all its non-human things first, and the created man, and accepting also that the non-human world functioned in a "Perfect" way from the beginning, it is not difficult to see why God would have wanted to interject mankind into this perfectly functioning universe, albeit a universe that is monotone, predictable, unfeeling and lacking the inner power of innovation and the power of change. In other words, the universe before man was "Boring" and "Stagnant". So God, seeing the futility of supervising a collection of his creations for ever, and needing to intervene to effect the slightest change and excitement and wonder, and knowing full well that he needed to create yet one more "Thing" that will forever relieve him from intervening in the course of his universe, decided to create Man. And God decided that with the creation of this Man and his descendents, God will have to dissolve himself in this new creature, and in order not to replicate himself and create the same dilemma all over again, God decided to give Man all the Godly qualities and powers less one: Perfection. For only God is perfect in every way, and it is this absolute perfection in his being an his ultimate wisdom that he created us and made us inherit qualities that he did not accord, in their totality, to any other of his creatures. And thus we are all Gods in our own right, however with no title to the Godly nature of our Creator except those qualities that collectively make us his Children and the inheritors of his Kingdom.

What a beautiful and wise act for assuring eternal perpetuity. God is here but he is not here. He is here because we are here. He is here because we understand in our hearts first, and our minds second that HE is imbedded in each and every one of us. Every newborn is another sign that God made the right decision.

Why then, people may ask, did God who is all "Perfection" and "Goodness" create in us this imperfection that makes us in certain cases do good and other cases do bad things? The answer to this question has to revert back to the way it should be asked. God did not create us to do good or bad. He simply created us with the ultimate freedom to be creative, and invariably anytime one speaks of freedom it should be in the absolute sense, without limitations to doing neither good nor bad things exclusively. It would be ludicrous to ask the sun to be always doing good for all living things. For as the sun is absolutely necessary for life, it also has the power to inflict bad things on the same creatures it nurtures. A gentle breeze we enjoy and depend on to carry pollen from tree to tree can become a hurricane that can destroy the same trees and wreck havoc with the same things it benefited when it moved at slower speeds. The same bacteria our digestive system depends on to nourish us can turn into an epidemic that can kill millions of people in the blink of an eye.

Nothing in this universe is all good or all bad. Once we confine anything to one category or the other we doom it to stagnation an eventual extinction.

The same principle governs mankind's behavior. The proof is each one of us. Even the greatest philanthropists will admit to having committed bad deeds at one time or another. This does not make them evil, nor do their good deeds make them the perfect human beings. They too, just like every thing else in life, will have to be evaluated in the totality of their accomplishments. Even the worst serial killers throughout history had a certain kindness towards the people they cared about, and for whom they were benefactors without any shadow of a doubt. I am certain that Nero was loved by his children, or at least by his wife. Hitler had a mistress who even accepted to die with him in his bunker. Saddam Hussein is still loved by his family an his village people and even proclaimed as a hero in parts of the Arabic world. Conversely, people who have dedicated their life's work to helping other people had enemies. Even mother Teresa had her detractors and naysayers, and people who believed in their minds and hearts that she must have had an ulterior motive behind her charitable works.

So where does this lead us in our relationship with God. Does he get furiously mad with those among us who are evil, or does he rejoice extremely in those of us who are good?

The answer is absolutely neither. The instant God gave us life and the freedom to "BE", he could not longer set any specific expectations from our behavior, neither good nor bad. However, since our most basic and fundamental driving force is to survive and better our lives, God's expectations are that we will generally strive to accomplish good things, even if along the way, some of us will undertake evil acts in the pursuit of accomplishing their own agenda at the expense of others. But is it not this basic pursuit of happiness that God gave us all? Some of us will seek their own happiness at the expense of others, and by committing acts that are deemed by the rest of us to be evil.

More to the point, we are inherently capable of this dual behavior, good and evil. It is not very uncommon to find even the best of us behaving in unnaturally evil ways towards certain people, under certain circumstances. Each and every one us has faced at least once in their lifetime the situation where, in the presence of people we do not like (Or even hate), we were forced to commit one of the most prevalent acts of evil, lie. Have you ever told someone you hate or cannot stand that you hate them or cannot stand them in their presence? Even though it really ate at you from the inside to be in the same room with them? I will elaborate on the subject of lying later on, but for now I will use it as a simple example to illustrate that human beings, contrary to all other creatures, use lying and deception for pure and simple survival purposes, and perhaps at a deeper level for perfectly justifiable reasons, dealing with and keeping this world civil and tolerable, but above all for making life in this world "Livable" and manageable.

Let us take an interlude at this stage and examine one act humans commit every day, millions and billions of times, in order to survive. The simplest way to look at it is by observing our behavior towards the animal kingdom. Do we not kill land and sea creatures to feed ourselves? Some people will argue that God put these creatures on earth for our own use and comfort. Perhaps this is true, but has anyone looked at this from the animals' point of view? Some people will argue that we are of a higher purpose, and I basically agree with this argument, but God never intended for any of his creations to be classified on any scale of importance. God created all things to act in a "System", all in unison, every creature contributing its role in making sure that the universe is functioning as a coherent unit. Animals kill other animals; even plants kill animals in order to survive. Hut that is the only way they can exit and thrive. We, human beings, even though our early ancestors ate no meat for a long time, have adapted ourselves to eating meat and by inference justified killing animals for our own nutrition. Not only that, but we also mastered the art of raising animals for the same purpose. But here also, we show evidence of ambivalence towards certain animals, especially those that are deemed not suitable for our consumption.

This selective behavior on our part shows clearly that we are great manipulators of our own circumstances, and when we are pushed to protect the survival of our own species, we are capable of extreme creativity, even if some of it may be labelled as evil.

We practice this creativity at all levels. People who need a job will find all kinds of way to tolerate a boss they despise. Is this not "Lying" at its best? However, we should not expect anyone to be so stupid as to tell the boss off. And it is a stupid boss who thinks or believes for a minute that all his employees love and adore him or her. And by the simple act of accepting the employees lies and deviant behavior, the boss is committing a lie and an act of deviance of the highest degree.

I am not citing these simple examples to berate or look down on the human nature. I am simply making observations that any one of us should be able to make, if we just look at things the way they are. More over, I am making these observations to drive home a very central point of my belief, that God created us with all these qualities, the good ones and the bad ones, so we can make our decisions as best suits us.

I was born and raised a Catholic Christian. I had no choice in the matter. My Mom and Dad were Christians, so I was sent to a Christian school where they drilled into my head all the teachings they deemed I needed to become a "Good" Christian. As I look back at these early childhood days, I can clearly say that I was never taught that other religions were bad or not true. However, when you drill into a child's mind, for few years, that Christianity is a wonderful religion and its principles are good ones, you automatically have asked that child to arrive at his or her own conclusions that all other religions are not as good, and in certain cases even wrong and bad. It is just the human nature. Just as I believed that my native country Lebanon, not even the size of Kentucky, was the most important, the most beautiful, the most civilized, and the most honorable. Never was I taught that other nations were not all these things. But as you can see, the implications in a young child's mind are huge, until he gets exposed to other cultures, which was the case for me when I took my first trips to France, and then to England, and later when I immigrated to the United States. Oh what a shock to my belief system.

I have to admit that, in looking back at what I was taught about Lebanon, for the most part, the teachings were done in a way to instill in me a national pride and a sense of belonging to a beautiful and proud nation. I believed these things then and I still believe in them now, and I will always believe in them. However, as I or anyone else goes thru these stages in life, I started reformulating these belief systems in a more rational and logical way.

The same process needs to take place for all humans, if we are to reach a state of understanding of each others, and of allowing for different belief systems to lead us to the one and only truth about God.

And it is not thru religions, at least not the way they are constructed and taught.

Throughout history, religions were at the center of most major conflicts on earth, or at least those who waged wars, waged them in the name of religions. The sad fact is that we are still facing religious wars even in the twenty first century, in spite of the positive proof throughout history that none of the other wars resulted in clear and permanent victory. And how would these people reconcile the contradictions between the peaceful teachings of religions and their justifications for killing other people in the name of these religions? There are no justifications.

The fact is that no wars were waged for religions' sake, they were always, and will always be waged for power and domination. If I want what you have, and if I cannot have it by peaceful means, I will wage war on you and take what you have by force. But when we do this, we always forget that just as we are the more powerful ones today, there will be someone more powerful than us tomorrow and they will inflict on us the same evil deed we have just inflicted on those who were less powerful than us yesterday. And so the cycle continues. Will it ever end, and will we ever have everlasting peace on earth?

Never.

I say never, because just as we are very smart and inventive, we are also very stupid in thinking that the world has limited resources, and that the God who created us for the noblest purpose would have put us in a situation where we lack the most basic resources to live and thrive. It is only thru our insecurities that we paint images of dwindling resources, which in turn feeds our sense of need to corral whatever resources we believe are available as our own. Surely there have been famines and extreme shortages throughout our recorded history, and surely there has been misery, hunger, deprivation and much suffering, but the irrefutable evidence is here in front of our eyes: We have survived and prospered in spite of all this.

Any rational being need only look at how much food is wasted every day in affluent societies to understand that, even today, with the population of earth approaching seven billions

(And by the way, we have not made or created any more land than the original earth), we are not only able to feed the majority of us on a daily basis, but we also throw away much of what the earth gives us and what we produce. The reality is that there is enough of everything to go around, but it is our false sense of shortage and insecurity that keeps us wanting to take care of number one, at all costs.

And it is for this reason that we shall never be at peace, complete peace, and for this reason that we have always lived in a "Relative" periods of peace. For one reason or another, we never seem to learn that no one wins in a war. Even those who are declared "Winners".

It is true that if it were not for our ingenuity and inventiveness, for finding ways to wrestle more out of the natural resources, and for bending nature's will to our advantage, we would have faced extreme and unspeakable shortages in food and shelter. But if this were the case, the obvious result of these shortages would have been either a decrease in the world's population or a slowing down of the population increase, to the point of equilibrium between our needs and our available resources.

Our history shows a definitive trend towards an increase in our numbers, at least as far we can tell. Perhaps the population of earth has never been this great, since we have no verifiable record of it either way. And maybe the population of earth had previously reached a greater number than we have today or even within the next millennium. Either way, there is no evidence that suggests we vanished due to the lack of natural resources. Recorded history points to mostly manmade events that wiped out great numbers of us, and at much larger scales than nature ever did.

The point being made here is that there is plenty of everything we need to go around. It is only our greed and selfishness that have driven us to behave in predatory ways, where we really did not need to.

Does this mean that we will ever reach a state of equilibrium, where we all have equal shares of everything? Absolutely not. It is the natural desire within us to always want more, better, and bigger things for ourselves that will always drive us to compete, and it is precisely this competition that fuels our development and the improvement of our lives. The problem with the way we have approached this is not in the magnitude of our acts, it lies rather in the manner we have approached it.

Throughout history, we have competed with our fellow men not in a way to demonstrate who is more capable than the other, but rather in a way that says to the others "I am right and you are wrong, I am good and you are evil, I deserve more and you deserve less, not because I outperformed you, but because I am the chosen one and I deserve the earth's riches, and you don't'".

We have turned our eyes and hearts and minds away from the concept of "There is safety in the numbers", not only that but there is goodness in the numbers. We have traditionally looked at others as a drain on what we have or want or need, and stopped seeing the truth that others are a prerequisite to our own existence and comfort. This can be demonstrated easily with few examples from our daily lives:

Suppose there were only one million people in the population of the United States of America, and the rest of the world had fewer people in the same proportional way. What do you think the price of everyday goods will be? How much would toothpaste cost? How much would we be willing to pay for some of the simplest comforts in life we have gotten accustomed to, like electricity, indoor plumbing, piped gas, and air conditioning? What would an average car cost if automakers had only a few million customers worldwide to sell to?

The list of everyday items we enjoy at relatively low cost is a long one. Some of these may be considered luxuries and superfluous to our most basic needs, but we have gotten used to them and to a certain extent we have configured our lives and economies around them. So now they have become necessities we cannot live without. It is not too hard to understand the power of our sheer numbers in making our collective lives comfortable. No one thinks on a daily basis about the upfront investment needed to come up with a new technology or a new product. Take the average car for example. We have been making cars, and good ones at that, for over one hundred years. So, one would assume that we have developed relatively cheap methods to come up with the next year's models. Wrong. It costs literally millions, and sometimes billions of dollars to release a new model. And car companies do not give this a second thought or concern, since they know that the ready market will allow them to recoup this investment, and to make a hefty profit too. If we assume all calculations were correct, and that each car will have to be sold for twenty thousand dollars, and we have tinkered with this model by removing half of the potential car buyers from the equation, but we will leave the same prospect for the auto maker to recoup his investment and make their predicted profit margin, it will follow that they have to sell each car they make for double the previously estimated sale price, or in this case for forty thousand dollars.

Now let us assume that the consumer base has shrunk to one tenth its actual size, each car will cost a whopping two hundred thousand dollars.

How many of us can afford these prices?

I a normal economic model, the forces at play will force the automaker to shut down its operations, since it could not raise the required investment for next year's model. Perhaps we would then be content to keep driving the same model for ever . . .

Lucky for all of us that there are so many of us around to make our economic model work, and work to our advantage. So, I need you, you need me, and we all need each other to make our lives enjoyable and comfortable.

Why then would some people want to get rid of others?

You are only good for a fleeting moment. The next moment, you have the obligation, if not towards the rest of humanity but at least towards yourself, to be a little bit better, or if you will a good bit gooder. It goes back to the original idea I expounded on earlier about perfection and how stagnant it make anything or anyone.

There is no perfection; there is only the pursuit of perfection. If God wanted to make us perfect, he would have done so from day one. He knew that perfect things are stagnant and boring and he could not deem us and his Kingdom to such a dreadful fate.

So God created us and entrusted in us the responsibility and the duty to keep reinventing ourselves, if not every hour at least every day. Those of us who reach a level of satisfaction with their accomplishments, and stop looking for ways to do things in different and better ways, and lull themselves in the false sense of "I have achieved all that I can achieve", are literally wasting God's gift to us. Not only that, but they are imposing on God a terrible sense of sadness and loss. Not because God benefits from our inventiveness, but he knows that thru our acts of ever-improving ourselves we improve life for all of humanity.

So, in the first degree, our responsibility is towards ourselves, for no one can start thinking of improving the lives of others until he has improved his own life. How could a sinking person rescue another sinking person? This may sound selfish, but that is the logic of life. If you have ever been on an airplane and listened to the safety instructions, you were told that in case the oxygen masks drop you are to secure your mask on your face first, and then proceed to helping a child put his mask on. It would be the height of stupidity to act in a macho manner and try to help others when you are yourself in need of help. And so it is with everything else in life. Whether it is an inner peace that some of us reach and help us get to a point of helping others because we have inner strength, or our ability to solicit help for others thru our own achievement of a certain status, we can never start helping others as long as we are in a position of weakness.

One would ask, what does improving oneself have to do with our purpose on earth and in the eyes of God? The answer is everything. For without us there is no life, and without us ever improving ourselves and our world we will all perish. I have a complete and unshakable confidence that neither will happen, at least not on a large enough scale to warrant concern.

It all goes back to the root of our psyche, and to the desire of most of us to preserve life by constantly solving daily problems. And here lies the problem, in the word "Most". The problem with us is that a great majority of us, for one reason or another, get too busy with the details of everyday life to look inward and make the same decision the other great ones among us have made, to not accept the status quo, to not get comfortable with any level of achievement, and to keep pushing the limits of our capabilities and talents to new heights, every day.

You may think this is an impossible feat, certainly for all of mankind. And I ask you: WHY?

Why can a Tiger Wood go to the driving range every day, for hours, even after he has reached the highest pinnacle of the game of golf? Why would YoYo Ma spend hours and hours rehearsing cello music he knows by heart in the first place?

The problem with our daily lives is that we tend to make them monotonous willingly. The receptionist who goes home after eight hours of fielding phone calls from callers to the office, goes home at the end of the day with one goal in mind: To leave all that behind, at the office, and just go home to relax, have dinner, watch some TV and go to sleep. The factory worker, after spending mind-numbing monotonous hours repeating the same task over and over again, can hardly wait until he gets home to engage in the same routine as the receptionist: Relax, eat dinner, watch some TV and go to slep.

We all wake up the next day to repeat the same sorts of things all over again. No wonder we start feeling like we are being used, like we are machines that are required to run and run and run and generate profits for the business owner.

_____

_____

_____

_____

_____

We are the only creature of God that knows for sure it will die one day. Perhaps certain animals and other living things know this by instinct and may look as if they are preparing for their death, but man is the only creature that knows this certainty with all of its implications at a different, deeper, and higher level.

Just like all other creations, we assure the survival of our species by procreating and multiplying, which comes very naturally to all living things. However, humans think about their death and eventual departure from this world in a more rational way, and take certain actions to perpetuate their lineage after they are gone.

We teach our kids our ways of life, because we want to preserve them. We write living wills and trusts to make sure that whatever we worked all our lives for, stays the course. As if we have this innate strong desire to bend the will of nature our way, when all other living things do not busy themselves with such mundane acts, yet their progenies live on and survive.

For some unknown and yet unexplained reason, we have come to believe in the after-life, and we have convinced ourselves that we need to arrange things and affairs in a certain way, if we wanted some kind of perpetuity and continuation of our earthly existence to keep on going after we are gone.

There is absolutely nothing wrong with this behavior, as long as we are not under any illusion that we will have a permanent and unchanging impact on the way we left things. History has shown and proven that whatever we do during our lives, whatever accomplishments, discoveries, inventions and other feats we leave behind, will always be subject to alterations by those we leave behind. Some will be for the better, others will be for worse. The main point we need to keep in mind is that once we are gone, we have lost control, period. It will be up to those we leave behind to rearrange the order of things in any manner that suits their purpose.

So my dear friends, we need to let go of the notion that there is an after-life and that one day we will come back or get resurrected from the dead. These are very comforting thoughts, if we want to believe in them, but I have yet to see irrefutable evidence that anyone, and I mean anyone, has ever come back to tell us how it is in the other world.

Christians believe that Jesus died and was resurrected on the third day. I cannot say what other religions think about this in private, but I can tell you that behind closed doors they reject, and some laugh at the whole idea. I don't reject it or laugh at it; I just don't take it in the literal sense, as the church wants me to. As I noted before, faith does not need reason to explain itself. If Jesus indeed died in the same way we know death for the rest of us (And so far, none of us has ever come back from it) how come he never left word describing what he saw in some details? Why is Jesus so much favored by God than the rest of us? Why did he talk about God and the other world and the kingdom of his father before he died almost exclusively while he was alive than after he rose from the dead?

It is so clever for all religions to accord their prophets and messiahs a mysterious exit from this world. And why not just say that these people, as holy as they may have been, passed away just like the rest of us but left behind a treasure trove of wisdom, love and charity? What are they afraid of? That we find out these people were humans like ourselves? That we would not believe in their message anymore? I would have more admiration for a human who has enough courage and sanctity for what he can accomplish for all mankind, more than if he were of Godly nature. People who possess supernatural and awesome powers are expected to accomplish great things, but it is far more incredible for normal and everyday people to accomplish great things.

This is why WE are here. To make sure the GRAND PLAN is executed by each and every one of us, and that the GREAT EXPERIMENT God has started will go on for ever and ever. Only through constant and deliberate acts of self-improvements that we can ever hope to be truly God's inehritors of his kingdom.

CPSIA information can be obtained at www.ICGtesting.com
Printed in the USA
LVOW080856110213

319249LV00004BA/269/P